I0813135

SPACE OBJECTS

STARS

by Elizabeth Andrews

Cody Koala
An Imprint of Pop!
popbooksonline.com

Hello! My name is
Cody Koala

This book is filled with videos, puzzles, games, and more! Scan the QR codes* while you read, or visit the website below to make this book pop.

popbooksonline.com/stars

*Scanning QR codes requires a web-enabled smart device with a QR code reader app and a camera.

abdobooks.com
Published by Pop!, a division of ABDO, PO Box 398166, Minneapolis, Minnesota 55439.

Printed in the United States of America, North Mankato, Minnesota.
102024
012025

Cover Photo: Shutterstock Images
Interior Photos: Getty Images, NASA, Shutterstock Images
Editor: Grace Hansen
Series Designer: Victoria Bates

Library of Congress Control Number: 2024938612

Publisher's Cataloging-in-Publication Data
Names: Andrews, Elizabeth, author.
Title: Stars / by Elizabeth Andrews
Description: Minneapolis, Minnesota : Pop!, 2025 | Series: Space objects | Includes online resources and index
Identifiers: ISBN 9781098246990 (lib. bdg.) | ISBN 9781098247553 (ebook)
Subjects: LCSH: Outer space--Exploration--Juvenile literature. | Stars--Juvenile literature. | Solar system--Juvenile literature. | Astronomy--Juvenile literature. | Universe--Juvenile literature.
Classification: DDC 523.8--dc23

Table of Contents

Chapter 1

Sky Sparkles

Stars look like tiny dots of light in the night sky. But they are actually giant, hot, glowing balls of gas! The most well-studied star is the Sun.

Watch a video here!

Milky Way

A solar system is made up of a star and all the objects that orbit it. The Sun is the star in our solar system.

Our solar system is in the Milky Way **galaxy**. There are 300 billion stars in the

Milky Way. Besides the Sun, the closest star to Earth is **light-years** away.

Chapter 2

Studying Stars

Stars come in different sizes and colors. The color of a star depends on its **temperature**. The size of a star is harder to determine. Scientists have many ways to study stars.

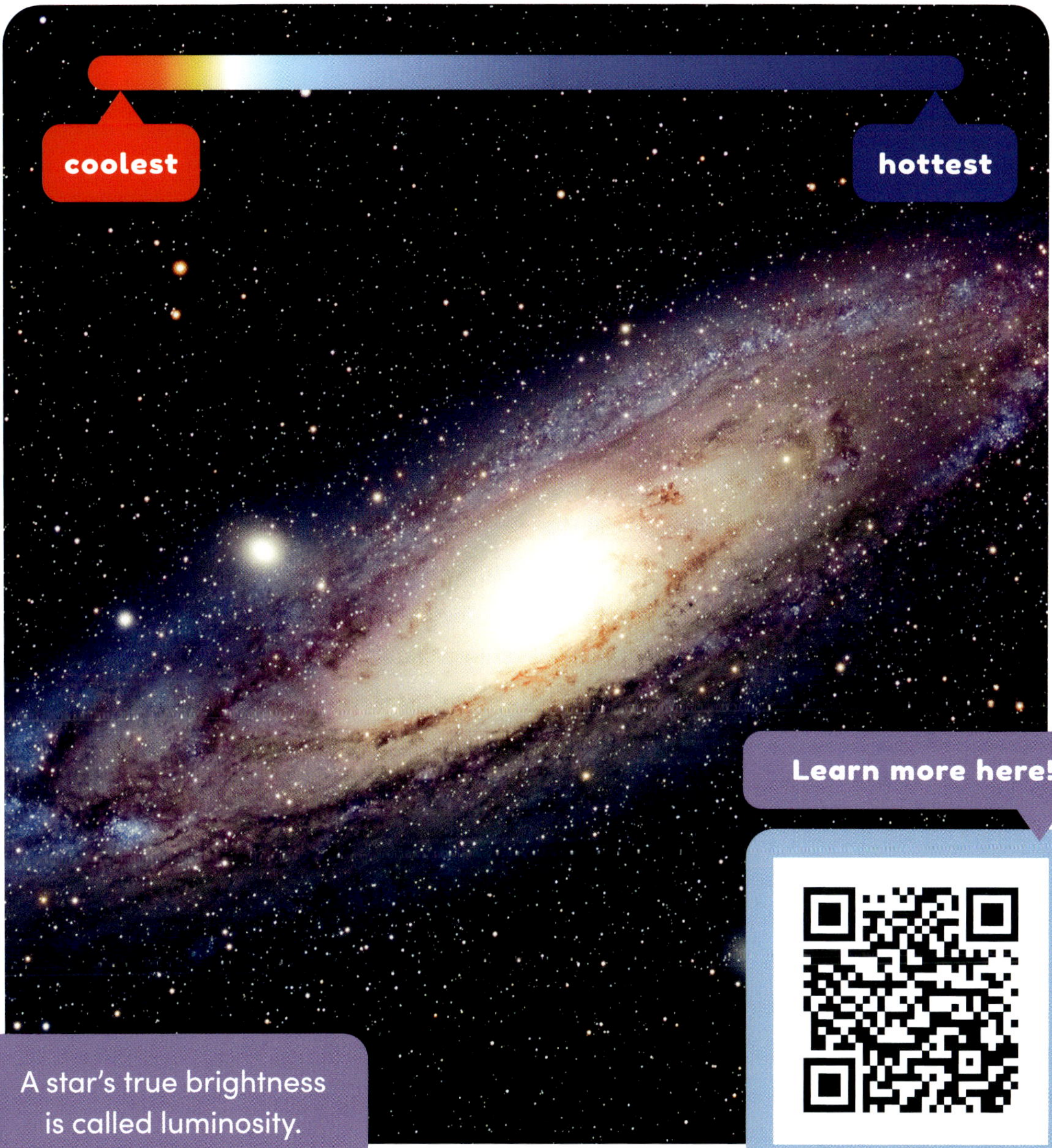

coolest

hottest

Learn more here!

A star's true brightness is called luminosity.

Chapter 3

Birth of Stars

Stars are made in spinning clouds of hydrogen gas and dust called nebulas. **Gravity** pulls gas and dust together into clumps. Clumps grow and become protostars.

Explore links here!

The core of a star is at its center.

For tens of thousands of years, the protostar spins faster. **Pressure** and **temperature** increase in its core. Inside the core, **nuclear fusion** occurs. This gives the star energy. The protostar becomes a main sequence star!

A star spends 90% of its life as a main sequence star. It glows as it burns through energy. Stars in this stage are different sizes. There are dwarf, giant, and supergiant stars.

The Sun is a main sequence star.

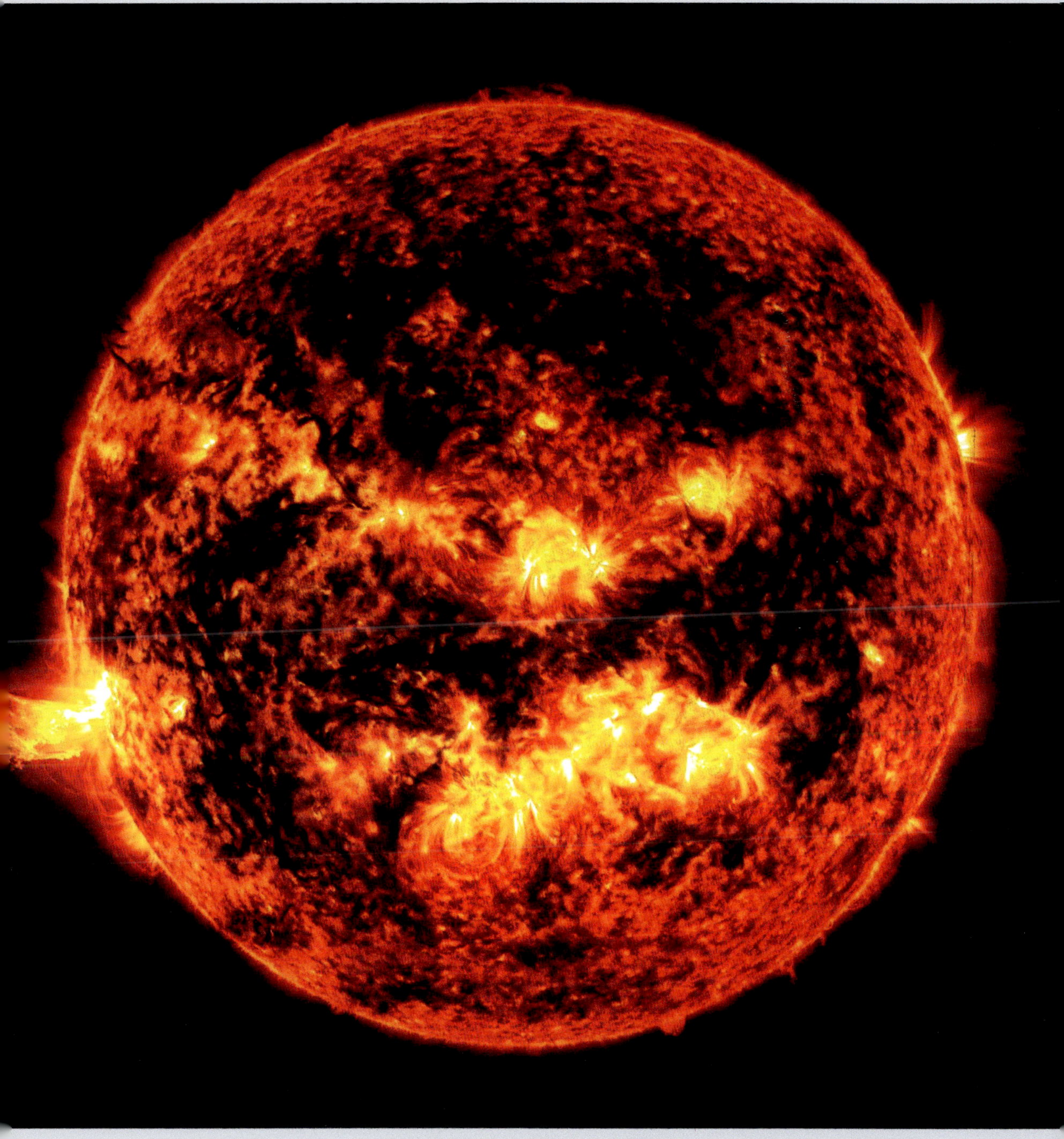

Chapter 4

Death of Stars

Stars live for billions of years. At some point they begin running out of energy. Their cores begin to **collapse**. What happens next depends on the size of the star.

Complete an activity here!

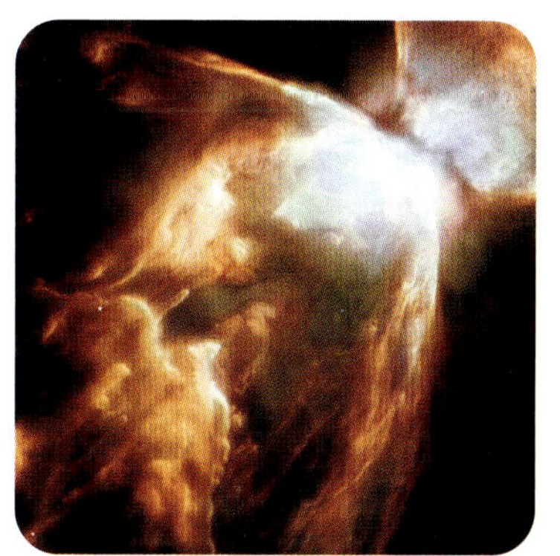

The outer layers of smaller stars spread and cool down as their cores collapse. Stars in this stage are called

planetary nebulas. Smaller stars fade into white dwarfs. When they are totally cool, they are black dwarf stars.

THE LIFE OF A STAR

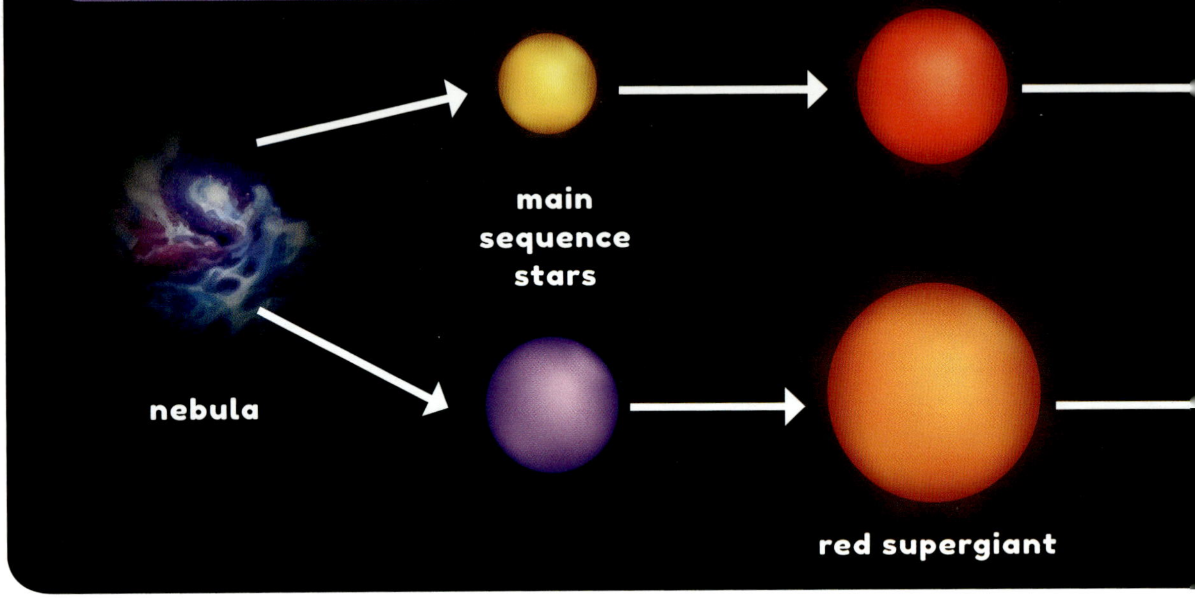

red giant

main sequence stars

nebula

red supergiant

Supergiant stars explode. The explosion is called a supernova. Then the stars turn into neutron stars or

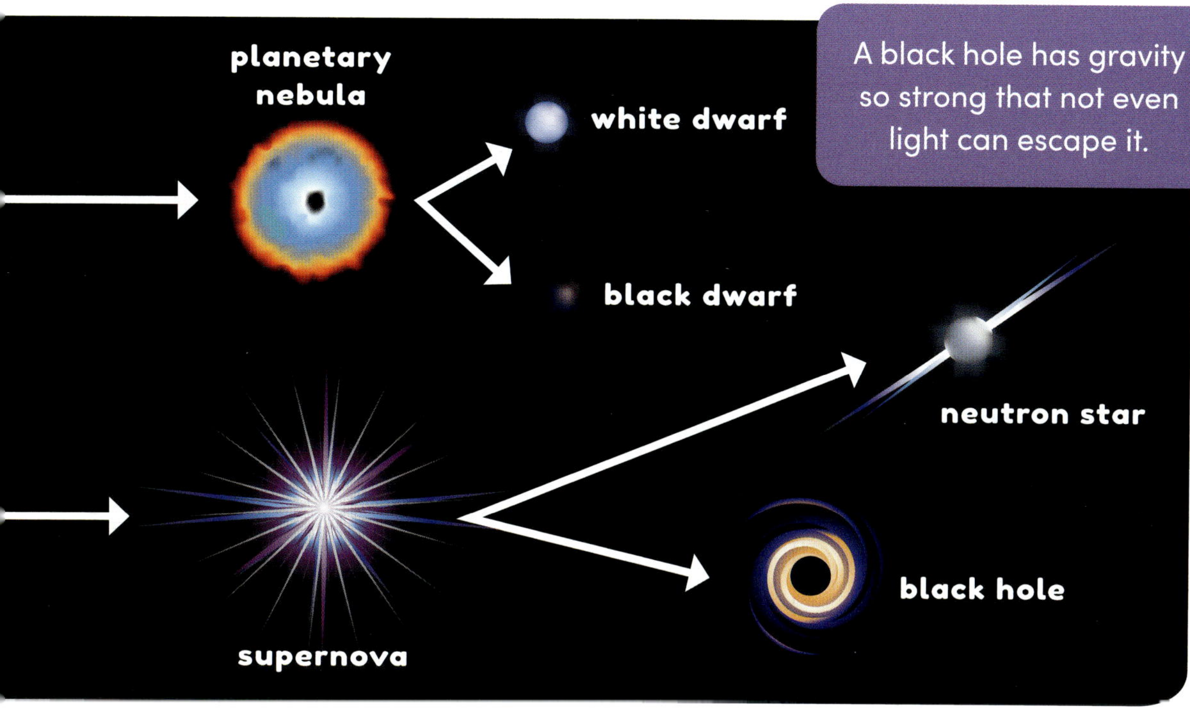

planetary nebula

white dwarf

black dwarf

A black hole has gravity so strong that not even light can escape it.

neutron star

supernova

black hole

black holes. Black holes are space bodies with very strong **gravity**. Nothing can escape them.

Making Connections

Text-to-Self

Which stage of a star's life are you most interested in? Please explain your answer.

Text-to-Text

Have you read any other books about space objects? If so, how were those objects similar to or different from stars?

Text-to-World

Sirius is the brightest star in our night sky. With the help of an adult, research Sirius's age, color, and distance online. Write a few sentences about what you learned.

Glossary

collapse – to cave in on oneself.

galaxy – a collection of billions of stars and other matter held together by gravity.

gravity – a force that pulls objects toward each other.

light-year – the distance light travels in one Earth year. One light year equals 5.9 trillion miles (9.5 trillion km).

nuclear fusion – a process that happens when two nuclei join to form a single nucleus. In stars, hydrogen nuclei fuse to make helium.

pressure – the amount of force on a certain area.

temperature – how much heat is in something.

Index

Online Resources

popbooksonline.com

Thanks for reading this Cody Koala book!

This book is filled with videos, puzzles, games, and more! Scan the QR codes* while you read, or visit the website below to make this book pop.

popbooksonline.com/stars

*Scanning QR codes requires a web-enabled smart device with a QR code reader app and a camera.

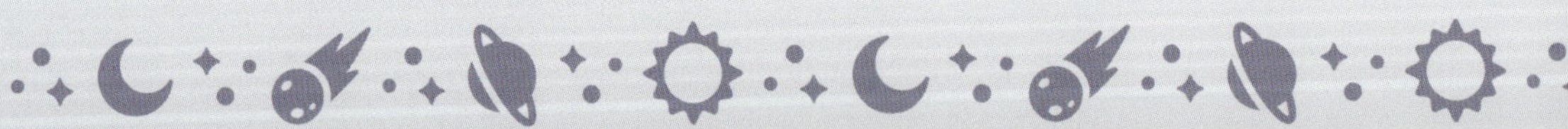